CONNECTING TO ABUNDANT SOURCE OF POWER

*This is not merely a book. It's a self-programming powerful tool, especially for youth to overcome any situation and emerge as an icon of success.

*After reading this book one will feel well-equipped, full of resources, having straight approach to the originator of all resources.

Each word, a pack of sense.

Dr Gajender Singh

CONNECTING TO ABUNDANT SOURCE OF POWER

HIGHLIGHTS

- A 'Powerful Tool' for emerging youth in any field.
- After reading this book you will never feel lack of resources.
- There will be abundant bubbling energy in you.
- You will be able to tap and use unknown/ hidden resources.
- This book is going to reveal the secret of complete success.
- The parameter of true success is not only money but also peace of mind, fame, relationship and time to enjoy; all these are equally important.

ABOUT THE WRITER

Hi!

Respected Readers,

I'm a retired Telecom Engineer from Indian Army, Doctor of Astro Science, A student of Brahma Kumari's Spiritual University. I was born and brought up in a small village of Rajasthan, India. Apart from schooling, much of my education was completed in the lap of nature. Jungle, River, Farms, Fields, Mounds, Terrains, Wild and Pet Animals; all these provided me a wide variety of education in practical which I studied in school in several books like science, humanities and business.

One important phase of my education happened to be in Delhi. Since my father was also in Army and was posted in National Capital, our family had a chance to be with him. There, I came to know, what does a defender mean. What is the meaning of unity and integrity? My perception went a step forward. I started thinking about world peace, prosperity and integrity. Apart from school, one part of my education was weekly movie.

All my previous scenario led me choose Army as my career. I served as a deterrent power to my country for twenty years. For several years I served as Unit Instructor and helped preparing my colleagues for United Nations Peace Keeping Missions.

World peace, fraternity and prosperity have been my vision of great interest. I'm still trying to spread humanitarian values and prosperity around. This book "CONNECTING TO ABUNDANT SOURCE OF POWER" is also a step towards this mission. I'm sure, you will not only enjoy reading it but also to prosper yourself.

Wish you all the best and happy reading.

----- Dr Gajender Singh

INTRODUCTION

This is a short, sweet and sure shot book to set a great combination of freedom, power, humbleness and success.

It makes a miracle to happen, to position you for what you want to get out of your life. When we are born, we come in this world with certain powers. People of this world, our kith and kin give us recognition with our health, color, shape and smile.

When we start growing, they give us recognition with the way how quick we learn to respond, how quickly we learn the things. Actually, in the primary stage of life, it all depend upon IQ and Sanskars we are carrying with us.

In the next stage of development, it all depend upon the parentage. They support us with their capacity and want to see us grow well.

In the next stage we start going to school and our life is molded by our teachers and friends. We play, study and learn with our friends and classmates. By this stage our self-learning process also start developing.

We start knowing our capabilities in comparison with our friends and classmates. Since we have a fixed IQ and certain background to support with, our growth rate is fixed. The life becomes monotonous. Many of the teenagers start searching for other fantasies and recreation.

This is the high time to get connected with the spirituality and tap the unknown powers available to us to cross the limit of IQ and physique. This book is all about, how to connect up to the source of abundant powers and how to make a successful life in the field of own interest.

<u>A NOTE OF THANKS</u>

First of all, I'm thankful to Almighty who is the ultimate guide to the whole universe. Secondly, I want to thank my parents and grandparents because of them I got a natural inclination towards the Infinity. I'm thankful to my teachers, friends, family and all the people I came across who made me learn something. Thanks to the writers of scriptures and the writers of books, of science, humanity, religion, spirituality, material and immaterial; I have gone through. Thanks to Maharshi College of Vedic Astrology, which made me learn about the importance of huge universal bodies like Sun and Moon to small stones like Ruby, Sapphire, Emeralds. Thanks to the scientists and technologists who made me realize that even in the smallest particle of the matter, the electrons, protons and neutrons are so perfectly placed and regulated that they stay well organized until and unless they are tempered. This is a different issue that these small atoms may be converted into atom bombs if tempered with. At last but not least, thanks to Brahma Kumari Prajapati Vishwavidyalaya which helped me brush up and align all this knowledge.

Note: This book is not to abandon life knowing spirituality but to make life a big success and celebration.

CONTENTS

9. Making life SUCCESS, Ours' and Connected Peoples', Giving SAKASH to all.

10. LIVE NIRVANA, An Achievement Beyond Imagination.

1. RECOGNISING ONESELF AS 'SOUL'

Different people have different recognition to the word SOUL. Some people are afraid of this word. Some people compare this word with Ghost, Spirit or those who are no more.

The fact is that Soul or Atman is the very essence of this body like having a number is very essential for a mobile. Without a number or code or a frequency a mobile is inoperative. Without the Atman a body is inoperative.

(a) RECOGNISING THE SOUL BY BIRTH

Soul builds up the body with the help of it's invisible faculties. While I'm talking about invisibility, I'm not talking about a vague. It's just like mind is the invisible form of brain. Atman has it's invisible faculties like Man, Buddhi, Sanskars and Smriti (Psyche, Intellect, Impressions and Memory). Of course, the memory is blank at the time of birth.

Many people think that the body is built up by genetic material provided by his or her parents. Yes, partially true but the complete truth is that a body is built by Soul otherwise a lot of genetic material go waste every now and then.

An ovum and sperm combination take shape of an embryo only when Soul enters the combination. It is the soul which attracts, collects, combines and arranges the material to form a body.

So basically, we are a well-motivated pretty energy (THE SOUL, a small part of powerful, infinite, Supreme Soul) assisted by our faculties; Psyche, Intellect, Impressions and Memory.

We just discussed about our initial stage of formation and preparation to come into this world, to recognize ourselves as a Soul or Master Soul which is the part, fraction or originated from the Supreme Soul.

To come to better understanding of this world, it's very necessary for us to understand this one step higher stage of this world, energy world, Soul concept or a programmed frequency concept.

When our understanding is one step higher, we have better understanding about this world. Since knowledge gives confidence, we are in comfortable position and our action in this world are more accurate, effective and progressive.

(b) RECOGNISING THE SOUL WHILE IT LEAVES THE BODY

As we had this example of the role of soul at the time of birth, we can have second example from the Soul leaving the body. What happens when biological age of the body is complete. What happens when the body becomes totally unfit to reside for the Soul? What happens when the Soul of a person is developed in the process and the body does not suffice?

In all the cases the Soul leaves the body and because the body was built up from the earthly substances as a vehicle to proceed on the path of self-development/development of the Soul; the body goes to earth and the soul goes to the Supreme Soul. Just as when a mobile is worn out, the phone goes to scrap and the number is stored back to Server.

(c) RECOGNISING THE SOUL IN OUR BODY

The next example to increase Soul consciousness is, if we observe our body, we see that we can live without many organs. We can replace many organs. Generally, some organ may stop working for some reason or ailment but they could be started again. While once the activity in the brain is stopped or the energy of the brain i.e. Soul goes out, no organ could work longer. Means the whole consciousness in the body is due to Soul Energy, remaining all the material is collected and arranged by the body as per Sanskars and DNA programming.

(d) HOW DOES MAN, BUDDHI, SANSKAR AND SMRITI WORK FOR THE SOUL

Man, Buddhi, Sanskars and Smriti (Psyche, Intellect, Impressions and Memory) are the manifestation of Atman, the Soul. Like a plot of land is manifested by various projections.

All these things further build up the desired body and senses. The aging and maintenance program also reside in Sanskars and memory, which is updated by senses and perceptions, in due time.

(i) Mann or Psyche

It is said to be the center of imagination, feelings and emotions. It has the power to show you green, prosperous, happy and positive sight of the future even when presently you are going through bad phase of life. The life seeming to be a hopeless desert, loss making business, worsening relationship, down troding social image…………… The worst thing is that some time you can't even show your bruises to anyone. Your Mann has the expertise to rescue you from such Gorges.

Another important field of your Mann is that it can imagine the situation one step further. It has the power to imagine unimaginable things and fantasies. Many of the researches are done by the power of imagination of our Psyche. It takes various fantasies further to the practical things. The data is supplied to Intellect which further analyses whether a particular imagination is possible or not and how?

Newton had a fantasy of apple. Why this apple came on ground? Couldn't it go upward and so on………

The data was further supplied to the Intellect and the laws of gravity came into existence. The way to go to moon and other planets was explored.

(ii)   Intellect

Intellect is the logical part of the brain or logical faculty of the Soul. It's like processor of a computer. All the logical work and thinking process is done here. It also provides coordination and connectivity among various sense organs, Memory, Sanskars and Psyche.

(iii)   Sanskars

Sanskars are the set of programs and habits like ROM, PROM and EPROM in a computer. Much of our routine work is done by the pre set programs which reside in the special memory called Sanskars.

The most interesting thing about Sanskar Memory is that we can reprogram many of the Sanskars by our awareness. We can get rid of the habits very easily. We can program it for fresh habits. All one has to do is to go in meditation feed pros and cons of the habit or Sanskar. Do it repeatedly for some time then bring it to Karmic level and repeat by awareness for some time, after a few sessions you will realize that it has become part of your Sanskars. This is also an effective way of getting rid of bad habits and formulating good habits.

(iv)   Memory

As it is very obvious from its name the memory cell contains a copy of whatever you see, hear, smell, touch, taste and perce. You can corelate with the pictures, Sounds, smells, touch feel taste and text.

When you see something pictorial, your memory corelate it with the sound file and you can tell someone else about what it was.

The same correlation is with the other senses, their reception and related files of memory.

(e) SOUL AND SUPREME SOUL

We must be assure that we all living beings are built up by soul, a specific energy or a programmed frequency which originates from Supreme Soul. That way we all have a big bonding. We all have same feelings. We all are pleased and sorry by the time and situation.

The first lesson we get being Soul Conscious is a feeling of humanity and brotherhood in this world. The second lesson is that our father (PARAM PITA) is very powerful, we can derive a decision, power and execution guidance with him.

The relation between Soul and Supreme Soul is like relation between Cell Phone and Server, like a PC and Server. The network Server is always connected and sending signals to the Cell Phone but the user can take desired advantage only when he recognizes, explores and uses the facilities available with the server. Alike things are there with the Soul and Supreme Soul. First of all, the Soul has to get introduced with itself. Many people just recognize themselves as a body. They are not introduced with their invisible part which manifested the visible part i.e. Soul. Once they are introduced with the Soul, they can easily be introduced with the Supreme Soul. When someone comes to know about when and how a mobile is live, he can easily imagine about the external link and concept of server. The same way our Soul also originates from the Supreme Soul.

(f) DISTRIBUTION OF POWERS BETWEEN SOUL AND SUPREME SOUL

Soul has limited powers and limited responsibilities. Like a stand-alone computer execute limited tasks only. Computer which is having a well knitted network with other PCs is more powerful but when it has internet connection, it becomes most powerful. When a Soul is well knitted with other Souls, it's having a group power. When it recognizes it's connection with the Supreme Power (Supreme Server), It's having ABUNDANT POWERS.

2. TAKING RESPONSIBILITY OF SELF CONTROL, SELF GOVERNING AND SELF RAISING

Of course, self-raising does not totally depend upon oneself. It has a copartner i.e. LUCK. But can we do something with luck? Nothing of course. So, we should focus on playing our part only.

Don't get overtired to abandon any task in hand. When a child makes efforts to stand up but can't maintain his balance repeatedly, he just has to look at his parents and the help is extended immediately. In the same way just the remembrance of Supreme Soul is enough for you to be helped.

Since we have recognized ourselves as a Peaceful Soul assisted by brain. Along with the development of the Soul, we have to be cautious not to take in the worldly vices and pollute our Soul. Much of the time we have to be under guidance and in connection with the Supreme Soul.

Further, we can control our life through our speech and behavior curated at the brain level through meditation.

(a) MEDITATION

Thinking about the word meditation, generally people think about uttering some words or mantras and all. It may be useful in some way but this isn't Meditation.

Meditation means sitting yourself with your Body, Mind and Soul. Have a peaceful, comfortable posture. While you are calm, cool and comfortable; you can have a very fruitful talk with yourself.

(B) SELF-GOVERNING

You can have the answer of any unanswered question. You can solve any unsolved problem. Trust yourself that you are in most powerful state of mind at this time. You are in such a powerful state of mind that you can give effective command to your Sanskars and habits to erase the bad one and create the better one.

(C) SELF-RAISING

You have a powerful and high-tech lab with you. It's well-fortified, secret and private enough to be sabotaged by anyone. No one can steel or temper with your data.

In the second phase of meditation you establish connection with the Supreme Soul, Abundant Source of Power, Energy and Wisdom. He keeps running your various body systems even when you are not in awareness about them. We have to give recognition to him. Meditate about him. Connect to him. Be able to get his blessings. Get his abundant power and guidance.

3. RECOGNISING OWN POWERS AND LIMITATIONS

Until and unless we are connected with the Supreme Soul, our powers are quite limited. The super most power of our Soul is our brain.

(A) BRAIN AND PHYSIQUE

The brain mainly consists of Psyche, Intellect, Impressions, Memory, Hypothalamus and Pituitary. There is another division also viz. Conscious, Subconscious and Semiconscious mind.

Brain has the ability to assess the situation, solve the problem, learn and express. All the internal systems are controlled by brain. Brain controls the sense organs. It stores and uses the information supplied by the sense organs. Brain controls the speech and body movement. All the physical abilities also depend upon brain.

(B) PARENTAGE

After Brain Power and Physical Functionality, the second most power on this earth is our Parentage. They support us to grow from very beginning. Their socio-economic level, intellectual level and attitude affect us a lot. More than providing food, clothing and shelter, they provide us with the Sanskars which further strengthen our position in the society.

(C) SCHOOLING, SOCIETY AND SOCIAL STRATA

Learning basics from home the child embarks to school. There he joins the kids of his age group. There he interacts with his teachers, schoolmates and society kids back from school. He is continuing to explore and learn the worldly wisdom. Hence the schooling and society play a great role in built-up of a person.

(D) ABILITY TO SERVE

After completion of education, everyone is full of knowledge and vigor. Of course, his serving ability depend upon his level of knowledge, service attitude and general behavior. Merely having degrees is not enough. Service providing attitude will work together.

All the above-mentioned things although serve as strength to a person, these may also indicate weaknesses while in comparison with person to person.

4. RESPECTING OTHERS AND RESPEECTING SELF

We may have achieved laurels in the field of knowledge and degrees until and unless we put it into public service in some way it's of no use.

Putting our knowledge into services means practically respecting others and earning respect. Everyone in this world has his/her self-respect. So we always have to maintain the dignity of everyone. There are various decorum to maintain the dignity of each one.

(A) ELDERLY RESPECT

Although we may directly be connected with the Abundant Source of Power but to have his blessings, we have to try our best to be in coherency with the channel. We have to respect the age at first. Whether a junior, poor or downtrodden, the age factor makes them a senior Soul, hence to be behaved appropriately. After the age factor it comes the experience.

(B) EXPERIENCE

May be that an executive has come on the chair after a lot of education, hard work and from a rich family but a worker, working in that environment for years has a lot of knowledge to be useful. If he gets a good behavior, he will prove to be more useful and comfortable to work for the organization.

(C) WEALTH

Anyone who is richer than us, may be because of his parents are rich and he has got the wealth for doing nothing but hierarchy. May be someone has got a lottery. There may be the people who seems to be doing nothing as hard work but has become richer by winning the election. We shouldn't have any scorn towards them. We never know how much hard work they must have put behind the curtain or through what condition or pressure they must have gone through. We just have to take their advantage if we can or leave them aside as they are.

(D) DESIGNATION

Sometime a very young man comes to a higher designation and we are startled. Certainly, he must have a good exposer to education and practical implementation. New generation is always prepared for the future. They come with advance learning, system and technology.

Some times they are given advantage just because of parentage but only a true talent will stay on. So being even lesser in age we must heed to what he says.

(E) Equivalents, Colleagues and Friends

Many a times we respect everyone even we don't comment or tease to those whom we consider to be in low grade but we often have a slack attitude towards our colleagues and friends. We think it's our right to tease them make fun of them and degrade them time to time. But we must get rid of this habit as soon as possible then we will be able to get mature only.

(F) Youngers → Juniors, downtrodden

It is seen many a times that a gatekeeper always salutes to his officers. A child always wishes good morning to his teachers, an employee always wishes good day to his boss but they may or may not get reciprocal response. Even they do not nod in reply. It's very easy to imagine to whom they must be more faithful. To whom they must have more confidence in. I'm not saying that you must salute them first or you must wish them first but it's their right to be reciprocated.

Likewise, when we favor some downtrodden, it must also be done with humility as part of our duty. Of course, we need not to go out of way to fulfil the need of someone which hard to afford for us.

5. TAPING THE UNKNOWN TREASURES

We may consume any amount of wisdom or worldly knowledge but our power is always limited until and unless we are connected with the abundant source of energy.

We have a limited GHz of processing unit or intellect, limited memory Bytes. We can only function right and function successfully when we are connected with Abundant Source of Power.

A STANDALONE COMPUTER has very limited powers. It is just like a typewriter. When the same computer is connected with the server, with the network, with the Internet it's power increases drastically. Rather than a TYPEWRITER it becomes an

INTERNATIONAL MACHINE to communicate with. In the same way a mobile is of very limited use if not connected with the server or network but when it is connected with the server or network, it acquires the efficiency to handle multiple type of communication. Handling not only calls but text, email, video, business, bank, presentation, conferences, worldwide.

Another example of taping the treasure is to connect up with the higher level of consciousness. In even today's world there are remote, tribal and very backward homosapien habitats. Their children play and learn together the art of Living and Survival but when they are connected with an organized learning system of Gurukul or some sort of schooling, they have a drastic change in their life style.

Likewise, there are several employees in an institute but those who are in touch with the policies and rules by the time and are well updated, go straight forward with the development of the organization. They not only cause to develop their organization but also have a good self-development.

Taping the unknown treasure is possible only when we come in union with a supreme power, person or organization. We have learned from several stories saying "Union is Strength". So first of all connecting with Superiors, having some kind of knowledge and power then distributing it to the lover entities will make you achieve success and get laurels in life.

Cosmos is eternal and our brain has the power and inbuilt instruments to be connected with the cosmos. Yoga is a technique to be connected with the cosmos. Many people have said and experienced that our brain has infinite possibilities to be used but we use only very less possibilities of our brain.

Now the question is how we as a Soul can get connected with the Supreme Soul or huge universal knowledge.

Here we go with the most wonderful part of this book which make us learn, how to tap the hidden treasures of the brain or how to connect with the Abundant Source of Power to make the best use of this life.

6. USING MECHANICAL WAVES TO CONNECT UP WITH THE HIGHER FREQUENCY/ SUPREME POWER

The best way to initially get connected with the Supreme Frequency is to start with the mechanical waves. Yes, as to learn any art, we need ample neat and clean space, peaceful and fresh mind, favorable environment. To learn to get a feel of that power, we also need the same at least in starting.

An early morning time as per your comfort is the best time for this, preferably morning 4 to 6. We have to sit in Padmasan, Sukhasan or any other sitting position in which you are comfortable. If someone is not able to sit in any of these positions, he or she could do it from any of his comforts or can directly start from the next method of getting connected, explained in the next topic.

Pronounce the learned frequency of Aum…….. for some time. After sometime, there will be a feeling of total peace, relaxation and pleasant confidence in mind. Now you may be assured that you are connected with your Server, The Abundant Source of Power. At what bit stream? Depend upon practice.

This is the high time for meditation now. You may bring in any question, you conclude a good answer of it. You may need to plan, organize or assess a situation, you will satisfy very soon.

In day to day life, we always have some questions which we can't ask with others or we do not satisfy what others answered. May be some planning also, long or short. May be the life is going smooth and we have nothing to meditate about but a synchronization is good to have once a day, preferably in the early morning.

Once our Soul and Brain is mapped with the Super Consciousness, we are ready to bear hustle and bustle of the day.

7. NEXT STAGE OF CONNECTING UP, USING BRAIN WAVES

In earlier stage we use mechanical frequency of Aum pronounced by our vocal cord which produce an effect of calm, cool, concentration and soothes the mind. The mind, body, Soul, Srishti and the Source of Srishti all come in unison. Every mystic thing or every un answered question seems to be crystal clear. It takes time to come to perfection by practice.

Now in the further stage we don't use mechanical waves rather we use improved version of waves that is brain waves. Brain waves are the same waves which are measured in the hospitals during an EEG test.

When we pronounce the sound Aum just inside our brain and don't utter by our mouth, we get the same effect as we get from mechanical sound of Aum produced by our vocal cord. Although it may be a matter of concentration. In learning stage if there is some problem to pick it, one may take a middle stage of pronouncing by the nostrils. Thereafter one may go easily to the brain waves. Both these techniques serve as sending the ring or pilot signal for connectivity.

The Supreme Soul is always connected to you, may be with a high or low bit stream during the hours of the day but when you are connected with him, you will feel elated, calm, soothing, pleasant and confident. This is called a both way communication in this condition you will most probably find the best answers of your questions. All the doubts and mystics fade away.

8. SUPER HIGH WAY TO CONNECT UP USING POWER OF SILENCE

After practicing the Brain Waves, the next level is super highway. The super highway connectivity uses power of silence. As the word suggest 'power of silence', there should be a complete silence or we have to be highly concentrated in Dhyana by closing our eyes. We should only have the image of Super Highway connectivity. The feeling of blessed, sheltered and supported will arise very soon.

This is like a hot line connectivity with the Supreme Power. This stage comes with the gradual practice. It can be used as a power dose even in the office for boosting the efficiency. Even a blink of few seconds is sufficient but we should regularly maintain the morning session. By regularly maintaining the morning session we have a power start of the day and by using Super Highway, we can have boosters during the day.

9. MAKING LIFE SUCCESS, OURS' AND CONNECTED PEOPLE'S, GIVING LIGHT TO OTHERS

Everyone in this world has limited powers. If we have to work more efficiently over to our inherent powers, we have to get connected back with our source of origin. Our source of origin is the source of Abundant Power, Knowledge and Wisdom. We may not only seek guidance for ourselves but also for our relatives and friends who depend upon us.

We wouldn't be able to enjoy the life in totality until we are surrounded by prosperous human beings. If the surrounding is not self survival, we always have to help them or carry their load. If the surrounding is stinking, its very difficult for us to be free of disease. If the surrounding is abusing and quarrelsome, we can't close our ears for long. So, along with our own life, we have to try time to time to touch the life of the people around us. In the language of Yoga, this is called giving Sakash. As in Bhakti Marg people utter the shloka –

"Sarve bhavantu sukhinah

Sarve santu niramaya

Sarve bhadrani pashyantu

Ma kashchid dukh bhag bhavet"

The same way in Yoga, we meditate with Supreme Soul to give peace, prosperity and fraternity around.

10. LIVE NIRVANA, AN ACHIEVEMENT BEYOND IMAGINATION.

While talking about Nirvana or Moksha people usually think that first of all we have to die and then our Soul has to be shifted to some another location or a confined area of abundance to attain Moksha or Nirvana.

May be true up to an extent but the real Nirvana is not the matter of place (Earth or Heaven), time (After Death or Before Death) or situation (Rich or Poor). it's the peaceful state of mind, an original state of Soul, well connected with its source, Generator or Supreme Soul.

The Moksha, Nirvana, eternal peace, joy and tranquility is a mantle status or a status of the Soul where it turns back to its Origin and Original Powers, which can be achieved anywhere in the cosmos, once we realize our original reality. Hence Nirvana is not dependent of whether you are in physical body, energy cocoon or even a pure energy.

Live Nirvana is a condition of total freedom from Maya (the illusions and sufferings of the world)/ Karm Bandhan. We achieve salvation while living on earth and being devoted to duty.

In this condition a person comes to realization of the world drama. He is clear in himself that in every situation, he has a best thing to do or a best role to play. This is what he can do only, since he has no more control further, so he is free after playing his part.

कर्मण्येवाधिकारस्ते मा फलेषु कदाचन ।
मा कर्मफलहेतुर्भुर्मा ते संगोऽस्त्वकर्मणि ॥

This is a great quotation from Shrimad Bhagwad Geeta. This quotation teaches us that a Karma (duty) with good intention is only what we have to do. It is not necessary that the result always be according to our choice. Neither we should take undue credit for that nor we should have any guilt for failure.

Nirvana can easily be achieved by continuously practicing Cerebral Yoga, Rajayoga or by practicing Soul to Supreme Soul connection. It is such a wonderful stage that the person achieving it, is always happy, satisfied and close to Almighty. He is never in debt for his Karmas to anyone. He is always having a clean chit from everyone. So, he is never worried about going upstairs. He is the achiever of such a great stage that he is quite happy being in this world and he is quite happy if called upon by the supreme boss. In fact, this situation is somewhat like a student belonging to a village family, works hard at his studies along with other choruses and quite cool in his village. The chance comes and he is called upon by a big university to join. He will be happy to leave his village and join the university.

There are times in everybody's life that he should step up and go forward otherwise the life becomes monotonous or the acquired knowledge and hard work seems to be in vain.

After achieving a particular level of worldly knowledge, having self-development and development of the Soul, one can live easily and freely in this world as well as ready for greater responsibilities in the abode of God, the Supreme Soul.

<u>WISH YOU HAD A HAPPY READING AND READY FOR A PLEASANT LIFE AHEAD</u>

Rear-View

CONNECTING TO ABUNDANT SOURCE OF POWER

HIGHLIGHTS

- A 'Powerful Tool' for emerging youth in any field.
- After reading this book you will never feel lack of resources.
- There will be abundant bubbling energy in you.
- You will be able to tap and use unknown/ hidden resources.
- This book is going to reveal the secret of complete success.
- The parameter of true success is not only money but also peace of mind, fame, relationship and time to enjoy; all these are equally important.

www.ingramcontent.com/pod-product-compliance
Lightning Source LLC
Chambersburg PA
CBHW031430160726
47993CB00003B/1481